Be Kind, Not Nice

*How to Stop People-Pleasing,
Build Your Confidence and
Discover Your Authentic Self*

MARCIA SIROTA MD

 Part 4 in the Short and Sweet Guides to Life series

Permission should be addressed in writing to: ruthlesscompassioninstitute@gmail.com(416) 782-5452

Disclaimer: This book is designed to provide information and motivation to our readers. It is sold with the understanding that the publisher is not engaged to render any type of psychological, legal, or any other kind of professional advice. The content of each article is the sole expression and opinion of its author, and not necessarily that of the publisher. No warranties or guarantees are expressed or implied by the publisher's choice to include any of the content in this volume. Neither the publisher nor the individual author(s) shall be liable for any physical, psychological, emotional, financial, or commercial damages, including, but not limited to, special, incidental, consequential or other damages. Our views and rights are the same: You are responsible for your own choices, actions, and results.

Cover Design
Patti Knoles, Virtual Graphics Art Department
VirtualGraphicArtsDepartment.com

Layout
Ginger Marks, DocUmeant Designs
www.DocUmeantDesigns.com

ISBN13: 978-1540873651

Dedicated to Myra Tennenbaum

*Your spirit lives on
in the love
we feel for you
and the passion
you had for life.*

Testimonial Reviews

"We use words like kindness and nice every day without ever really thinking about what they may actually mean. By deconstructing two seemingly simple words in an attempt to define them, this book opens a doorway to a deep meditation on self-forgiveness, healing and true personal potential."

Jeff de Boer
Multi-media Artist, best known for Suits of Armour for Cats & Mice

"Every page of Dr. Marcia Sirota's new book reflects her own intelligence and compassion. Be Kind, Not Nice offers the kind of encouragement we all need — not rooted in fantasy or wishful thinking, but based in a truth that is unlocked with greater understanding of ourselves and our own potential. You are amazing, and Dr. Sirota can prove it."

David Hopkins
Writer and Author of *We Miss All The Great Parties*

"Fed up? Want to discover a new way? Be Kind, Not Nice offers valuable insights into how to have more happiness and joy in your life."

Michael H Ballard
Speaker, Trainer, Consultant

Contents

Introduction

This book explores the difference between being kind and being nice. These two concepts can be difficult to distinguish, but they must be, as they create very different outcomes in life:

Being kind creates connection, happiness and success, whereas being nice leads to anger, frustration, alienation, even addiction.

I've started this book by discussing where self-esteem comes from,
how you can get into a vicious circle of low self-esteem, and how you can improve your sense of self.

I set up the book in this way to make it clear how the difference between being nice and being kind lies in the presence or absence of good self-esteem; the nice person lacking it and the kind person having it in abundance.

The nice person is seeking (but failing) to build their self-esteem through having others validate and affirm them; the kind person is full of happy, positive feelings, and these spill over into their dealings with others.

The nice person tries in vain to meet their needs through pleasing others. Instead, they meet with frustration. What they don't realize is that these needs for validation cannot be met by someone else.

Our self-worth is our own responsibility, and no matter how much approval we receive from others, it's up to each one of us (with help, perhaps, from a trained professional) to develop this for ourselves.

Reading this book, you should learn how you developed, or failed to develop, good self-esteem; why you've been so "nice" all this time; and how, by rebuilding your self-esteem, you can go from being unhappily "nice," to being confident, authentic, and joyfully kind.

Chapter 1

You are Amazing!

You may not know it yet, but you are absolutely amazing.

Really, you're great!

You deserve the best life has to offer.

You have everything it takes to make your dreams come true.

You are lovable!

You really are!

If you find it hard to believe all this, it might be because of things that have happened to you,

or things that you've done, but you need to know that what you've experienced and choices you've made aren't a reflection of your worth.

You need to see that any trouble you have with self-worth is not a true reflection of your value or your abilities.

You were born with infinite potential.

You were born innocent and intact.

The struggles you've been experiencing aren't caused by incompetence or a lack of intelligence, talent or drive.

The struggles you've been experiencing are caused by your emotional wounds.

We experience these wounds in childhood.

They aren't our fault.

But they are our
responsibility to heal.
(More about this, later.)

In the best of all
possible worlds,

parents and guardians
love their children,
unconditionally.

They accept their children
with all their imperfections,
flaws, quirks and challenges,
because real love never
has to be earned;

it's given freely by those who
are able to love.

Good parents would
never do anything to
harm their children,
and they protect their
children from the harm
that others might try
to cause them.

If you're at all lacking
in self-esteem,
it might be because
you were loved
by your parents,

but people at school were abusive to you.

It could be that you weren't loved or protected enough as a child, or perhaps you were hurt by someone who was supposed to care for you:

Parents bring their history to their parenting.

If they were hurt, neglected or rejected in their childhood, their own emotional wounds might make them unable to love their children, unconditionally.

They might be so troubled that they harm their child, or fail to protect their child when the child is being hurt by the other parent or by someone else.

Sometimes, parents are so distracted by their own problems that they can't put enough

attention onto properly caring for their child.

(But don't worry · · · You aren't doomed to repeat the mistakes your parents made.

With help, you can heal your childhood hurts and become a great parent to your own children.)

The good news is that not all people who had difficult childhoods are so wounded that they can't love their children unconditionally.

Not all parents who had
difficult childhoods
are so troubled that they'd
hurt their child
or fail to protect their child
from harm.

And not every parent
with problems will
neglect the care of
their children.

Every person is unique,
and how they respond
to the hurts of the
past depends on their
own, inner make-up.

Some parents are more resilient; some are less so.

If you're lucky, your parents were able to love and protect you enough, and never harm you in any meaningful way, no matter what kind of childhood they had.

But, maybe your parents were so wounded by their past experiences that they weren't able to love you in the way all parents should love their children.

Maybe you had a parent whose emotional wounds caused them to be very hurtful to you; maybe you had a parent whose emotional wounds made them unable to keep you safe from harm.

Maybe you had a parent whose emotional wounds made them unable to connect with you.

If you belong to any of the latter three groups, you probably have low self-esteem.

Self-esteem comes from taking in all the love, acceptance,

affirmation,
encouragement and
protection you received
as a child.

It comes from
being treated with
respect, kindness and
consideration, and then
seeing yourself through
the loving eyes
of your parents.

It comes from
not having been
abused, neglected,

shamed, exploited or manipulated.

The more positive things you received, and the fewer of the negative ones, the better your self-esteem will be.

Conversely, the fewer positive things you received, and the more negative ones,

the more fragile your self-esteem is likely to be.

The most important thing to know is that

no matter how you were treated,

it wasn't about you.

Parents love (or don't love) their children, based on their own inner ability (or inability) to love.

Parents care for (or fail to care for) their children, based on their own inner ability (or inability) to care.

You **never** did anything
to deserve
neglect, abandonment
or mistreatment.

And you **couldn't** have
done anything
to get your parents
to love or protect you
more.

Love is the most
natural emotion in
the world.

We're hard-wired to feel
it toward each-other.

We're hard-wired to
care for each-other
Sadly, emotional wounds can
short-circuit our normal wiring,
making us less able to love.

When the hard-wiring
of our parents has been
short-circuited,
they're less able to
follow their natural
instincts, when it comes
to loving us and caring
for us.

Children are hard-wired to take everything personally.

In the best of all possible worlds, that would mean that all the love, care, affirmation and protection we receive would become our absolute truth.

We'd feel like we deserved this unconditional positive regard, and our self-esteem would be strong and healthy.

In the real world,
where some parents are
emotionally wounded from past
hurtful experiences of their own,
children respond to the lack of
unconditional love or protection
by feeling like **they must have
done something** to deserve this.

Our hard-wiring as children
makes us feel that the way
we were treated as children
really was a reflection
of our value.

We feel unworthy, inadequate,
or defective,

when what we need to
see is that · · ·

each one of us is beautiful,

and our value is not related to how we were treated while growing up.

You are a beautiful person,

and you need to know this, right now.

No matter how you were treated

as a child, you are a good person.

No matter how you were made to feel,

You deserve love and respect.

No matter what mistakes you've made,

You are valuable and lovable.

And you need to start believing it, now,

in part, so as not to repeat the cycle with your own children, and with the children in your family.

As you grow up, there are other influences on your self-esteem.

Your relatives, teachers, coaches, clergy and peers all have an impact on

how you feel
about yourself.

Incidents of bullying,
harassment, abuse or
exploitation by these and
other people
can leave you with
low self-esteem,
even if you had loving,
caring parents.

The media is a huge influence

in how you see
yourself.

*Images of what
is supposed to be
attractive, lovable and
good are constantly
portrayed in the
media.*

*The problem is,
these images usually
have very little
to do with*

what's **really**
*attractive,
lovable and good.*

It can be easy to develop
a complex about your
appearance, your abilities,
even your value as a person,

if you absorb a lot
of information from
magazines, TV, movies
and online.

You're going to have
to take what you hear,
see and read with
a big grain of salt.

The media, and lots of folks online, don't have a clue about how great you really are!

The messages you've taken in
about yourself,
from all these sources,
have a big impact on
your self-esteem.

To repeat, even with loving parents, other people you encounter while growing up can negatively influence your self-esteem,

and the media is constantly working to undermine your self-esteem···

(···in large part, to make you buy things to "help" you feel better about yourself·)

You can take responsibility for your own self-worth·

You can begin to feel so much better about yourself·

There are simple tools you can use to build your self-esteem·

I'll tell you all about them, shortly!

The story of Joelle*:

Joelle is a 30-something woman who is extremely smart, capable and resourceful. Sadly, because of their own emotional issues, her parents were unable to love her and appreciate her the way she deserved.

She was given many adult responsibilities as a young teenager, and even though she did a good job, her parents never acknowledged her talents or abilities.

Her mother was extremely critical, and her father always assumed that she'd fail. Joelle grew up with very little confidence in herself, even though she had many examples of her competence from her childhood.

Her parents' negative messages about her made it hard for her to acknowledge her own accomplishments. She couldn't connect her abilities with the positive outcomes, and she couldn't use her successes to boost her self-confidence.

Joelle never believed that she was lovable—Mom and Dad never made her think so- and she came to think that the only way to get people to like her would be to do things for them.

Joelle became a people-pleaser to the extreme. Eventually, she was surrounded by crowds of people, but unfortunately, all of them were using her, and taking advantage of her generosity.

As soon as she stopped being so helpful and useful to everyone, they all seemed to disappear out of her life. She realized that they'd only been with her because of what

she'd been doing for them, and that no-one really loved her for who she was.

Joelle lost all her false friends, and after a lot of soul-searching, she started psychotherapy and in time, this helped her to realize that she was now free to start making true friends. She was ready to learn that, despite how her parents treated her, she was lovable and competent, and that people could accept her for who she was, not just for what she did to please them.

Joelle was ready to learn that by no longer being a pleaser, she could start to attract people who'd be with her because they liked her, and not because of what she could do for them.

Chapter 2

The Vicious Circle of Low Self-esteem

You can begin to feel better about yourself.

It starts with seeing that you've been

trapped in a vicious circle of choices that keep lowering your self-esteem.

Here's how it works:

When you don't feel so good about yourself or you don't believe in yourself, you tend to do things in ways that reinforce these feelings and beliefs, and also interpret things in ways that reinforce these beliefs.

You choose not to try something, for fear that you'll fail···

but not trying something never lets you see that you could have done it; you could have succeeded at it·

In fact, the less you try, the more convinced you are that you can't do it, and the more you believe you can't do it, the less you try·

Of course, there are lots of
things you can do,
but when you're trapped
in this vicious circle
it can be really hard
to see this.

Self-doubt creates a self-
fulfilling prophesy:

When you doubt yourself, you
can get so anxious that you
make unfortunate mistakes-
mistakes driven by nerves.

When you make these mistakes,
it's easy then to believe that
you're not really competent.

So, whether you're not making
an effort out of fear of failure

or you're messing up because self-doubt is messing with your head,

all of this just reinforces low self-esteem.

Then, when you feel bad about yourself, you're even less likely to try something, and more likely to mess up, out of nerves.

The less you try things, the more you believe that you can't do them. This is, in part, because you've accumulated no real-life proof of your abilities...

and the more you mess up (because of your nervousness and self-doubt), the lower your confidence goes, taking your self-esteem with it on the way down.

What you don't see, and need to see, is that the majority of your mistakes are caused, not from incompetence, but out of your anxiety and self-doubt.

If you could let go of this anxiety and self-doubt, your performance would begin to improve, and you could manifest your true potential.

In fact, the greatest predictor of success isn't innate intelligence, talent or ability. It's self-regard.

If you think well of yourself, you'll do better, regardless of how smart or talented you are.

If you think poorly of yourself, you'll often do worse, regardless of

how smart or talented you are, and even if you're competent, it's unlikely that you'll be able to enjoy your success.

No matter what your innate level of intelligence or ability is, how you see yourself plays the greatest part in how far you'll go in life.

You can choose to believe that you're OK, or you can choose to believe that you're not OK.

Ultimately, it's a choice…

and you can learn to make the better choice.

Another choice that's common in people with low self-esteem is to

associate with others who perpetuate your lack of self-worth.

The more time you spend with those who put you down, exploit you or disrespect you, the worse you'll feel about yourself.

The more time you spend with such people, the less likely you are to try things, and so the less likely you are to succeed.

The more time you spend with these hurtful people, the

more likely you are to mess up, and the more likely it is that you'll feel bad about yourself.

These types of people are instrumental in undermining what little self-confidence and self-worth you had to begin with.

You'll become totally convinced that you're worthless, and grateful that the other person is willing to "tolerate" being around you.

These types of relationships, whether with a friend, family member or romantic partner, are **abusive,** as they convince you that you're no good, and that you're undeserving of happiness or success.

If you stay with these people, because you think that they're the only ones who'd want to be with you, you'll never get a chance to break away and heal your wounded self-worth...

or see that there are others out there who could treat you with respect.

It can become harder and harder to see that you're a good person

and that you deserve so much better than this.

And you do deserve better!

You deserve what every single person does:

to be your authentic self; to fulfill your potential; to live your best life.

You deserve to pursue happiness,

you deserve to be loved,

you deserve to be treated with respect.

Being with hurtful people distorts your sense of who you are and what you truly deserve.

Being with hurtful people perpetuates the vicious circle of low self-esteem.

Another thing that perpetuates low self-esteem is having unrealistic expectations of yourself.

It's unfair to expect yourself to be perfect, or to think that you "should" be amazing at something, the first time around.

The people who gave you low self-esteem in the first place also put these unrealistic, unfair expectations onto you.

They made you feel that they'd only approve of you if you were perfect; that you'll only be accepted if you accomplish impossible goals.

Since these expectations are impossible to meet,

you get to feel bad about yourself all the time.

The more you walk around with overly-high expectations of yourself, the more fuel you give to your self-criticism and self-doubt.

The more you take on challenges that are too big for anyone in your position, the more you (falsely) convince yourself that you're inadequate or incompetent.

The more you believe the (obvious or subtle) lies of the people who raised you or taught you; the lies that say you're only acceptable if you achieve the impossible,

the worse you end up feeling about yourself.

Fortunately, there's something you can do to break these vicious

circles and build your self-esteem.

Even if you feel really crummy about yourself, even if you've spent a long time avoiding challenges;
even if you've made a lot of unfortunate mistakes,

you can improve your self-esteem.

Even if you're surrounded by people who reinforce your low self-worth;

even if you've had unreasonably high expectations of yourself, **you can do it.**

But before we get into that, we need to look at a few other things that undermine your self-esteem.

Aside from these vicious circles, here are the other things that undermine your self-esteem:

guilt,

shame,

obligation,

self-blame.

These are all things you would have learned while growing up, from your parents, family or community.

Shame eats away at self-esteem because it makes you feel dirty and small.

Guilt erodes your sense of self because it makes you feel bad and undeserving of good things.

Obligation tears away at your self-worth because your value becomes connected to how well you've served the needs of others, or how poorly.

Self-blame destroys self-esteem because you're taking on responsibility for all the bad things that are happening around you.

All these attitudes are things that you were taught.

You don't have to hold on to them any longer.

You can let go of shame.

You can let go of guilt.

You can let go of obligation.

You can let go of self-blame.

The shame you feel has nothing to do with you.

It was just put on you, and it really belongs to the people who put it on you.

The guilt you feel just means that you were successfully manipulated.

You don't have to buy into this brainwashing.

The obligation you feel is more manipulation.

You don't owe other people anything more than your respect, courtesy and consideration...

and not even that if they're cruel to you.

Your self-blame comes from having been unfairly blamed for things that weren't your fault.

You can exchange your self-blame for an appropriate sense of responsibility.

Shame, guilt, obligation and self-blame are burdens you don't have to carry, any longer.

You can be free of these toxic assaults on your self-esteem.

The Story of Carly*:

Carly is a middle-aged woman who has spent her entire life struggling with low self-esteem. She grew up with parents who never really wanted children, and a mother who resented her for being a "burden." Carly's self-esteem never had a chance to develop.

Carly associated herself with a group of people for many years who were a lot like her neglectful and critical parents, and who reinforced her poor sense of self. Her career moved forward, but she avoided close personal relationships out of fear of rejection.

Carly never felt entitled to stand up for herself and tell people how she felt or what she needed from them. She avoided confrontation and tolerated situations in which she felt mistreated or disrespected.

Carly was a people-pleaser, who thought that if she was "nice," people would be less likely to treat her the way her parents did. Unfortunately, her niceness only caused people to disrespect her and take advantage of her.

Carly became upset at times, but was so afraid of abandonment that she never said out loud to anyone that she was getting angry.

Eventually, her resentment began to spill over in passive-aggressive behaviour and uncharacteristic outbursts of anger.

Her outbursts horrified her and made her feel like a bad person, and the passive-aggressive behaviour, as well as the angry outbursts, made other people upset with her.

All of this only served to further weaken Carly's fragile sense of self-worth. She became stuck in a vicious circle of low self-esteem, people-pleasing, resentment, leaking of anger, self-criticism, rejection from others, and further low self-esteem.

Fortunately, Carly sought help for her problems. Working hard on herself in therapy, she slowly began to see that the things that had happened to her in childhood were never about her, but were a reflection of her parents' limitations.

Carly slowly learned that she didn't have to please people in order to have good relationships with them, and when she began to let go of pleasing people, she was also able to let go of the resentment caused by this dysfunctional behaviour.

Carly's self-esteem began to grow, and she saw that she could be genuine in her interactions with others. She saw that some people would be able to like her for exactly who she was, and some people would never like her, but that this wasn't a reflection of her worth.

Eventually, Carly let go of her people-pleasing, as well as her resentment, and she became more authentic, happier, and more able to interact with people in a satisfying and meaningful manner.

Chapter 3

Building
Self-esteem

So how do you begin to develop good self-esteem?

It starts with five basic concepts:

Being loving to others, Being creative and productive, plus

Self-acceptance

Self-forgiveness

Self-compassion

It also involves good self-care, including:

self-nurturing, self-soothing, self-reassuring and self-healing.

Self-esteem grows through loving others: Being considerate, caring, generous and compassionate makes

everybody happier and makes you feel good about yourself.

Self-esteem grows through being creative and productive:

Building things, making things, generating ideas, collaborating with others, being involved in meaningful projects, engaging in community-building and world-improving activities all contribute to better self-esteem.

Paradoxically, self-esteem is supported by thinking less about yourself:

The more self-involved you are, the easier it is to focus on your short-comings.

The more you put your attention on other people and on the world, the less you think about yourself.

This will decrease your opportunities for self-criticism.

The more you focus on how you can make a contribution to others and to the world, the better you're going to feel about yourself.

This is indirect self-esteem building···

and it's pretty powerful.

Altruism is amazing for building self-esteem...

and not in a self-important way, but by creating a sense of loving connection to others that also makes you feel great about yourself.

Sharing, caring and belonging builds self-worth.

When you belong to a loving family, positive community or close group of like-minded people, your sense of self-worth grows.

The most important thing to recognize is that you are the one who's responsible for your self-esteem.

Only you can do the inner work to feel better about yourself.

(But you can get help, doing it!)

No matter how much someone else loves you, cares for you, takes care of you, they can't fix your self-esteem.

That's your job...

yours and yours alone.

Once you understand this, you're on your way to developing a really good sense of yourself.

Self-acceptance is a misunderstood idea.

It doesn't mean thinking that everything you do is fine.

It means that you see yourself as a good person and don't feel the need to fundamentally change who you are.

Self-acceptance is giving yourself what your parents and community should have given you:

unconditional positive regard.

Self-acceptance is not a free pass to misbehave.

It's not a "get out of jail free" card,
like in the game
Monopoly.

It's feeling that you're
OK, just as you are.

**And the truth is,
you are OK,
just as you are!**

When you accept yourself, you feel better about yourself.

When you feel better about yourself, you try more things and you become more competent.

Self-acceptance gives you the space to relax, breathe and just be yourself, so it's easier to achieve your goals.

Self-forgiveness is so important in building up your self-esteem.

Anything that you've done wrong, any mistakes you might have made, all these weigh heavily on you.

When you forgive yourself, you can calm yourself and regroup.

You're less anxious, so you do better.

Self-forgiveness stops the negative self-talk in your head, which tells you how "bad" or "stupid" or "useless" you are.

It creates space in your head for positive thoughts to enter.

Self-forgiveness is treating
yourself with
fairness and kindness.

You deserve to be treated with
fairness and kindness, always.

When you forgive yourself,
you feel a sense of inner peace
and ease.

Self-compassion is even more poorly understood than self-acceptance.

Self-compassion means wanting the best for yourself.

It's seeing yourself
and your choices with
complete honesty,
and striving to make
better choices;

it's understanding why you've
been stuck, and why you've
messed up.

Self-compassion is never
self-leniency; it's never
self-indulgence.

In fact, it's respecting yourself enough to know that with the right support, you can do better.

It's not pushing yourself too hard or giving up on yourself; it's believing in your own potential.

It's holding yourself accountable, but kindly.

Self-compassion enables you to see the best in yourself and enlist help to be the best you can be.

It makes you want to give yourself love, nurturing, soothing, reassurance and healing.

All of the above constitute good self-care.

Self-love is not the same as being selfish, self-important or self-centered.

Self-love is cherishing yourself, knowing that you're the most valuable person in your world, and that you must take care of yourself.

When you're filled with self-love, the love begins to overflow onto all the other people (and animals) in your life.

In this way, self-love is the spring that feeds your love for all other living beings.

Self-nurturing isn't spoiling or coddling yourself.

Self-nurturing is making sure that you're well, mentally, physically, emotionally, and spiritually.

When you nurture yourself with good food, rest, exercise, play, creativity, connections, meditation, self-pampering and

being in nature, as well as recognizing and celebrating your strengths and talents...

you feel better and better about yourself.

And you deserve to feel really good about yourself.

The more you nurture yourself, the better you feel about yourself; the better you feel about yourself, the more you'll nurture yourself.

And asking for help in all this is not only acceptable, it's recommended.

Self-soothing is so important.

Life is full of pain and hardship.

There's loss and disappointment, frustration and heartbreak.

When you know how to soothe yourself, you aren't tossed about on the waves of misfortune.

When you can soothe yourself, you have more trust in yourself.

This self-trust creates a sense of inner peace and confidence.

When you can't soothe yourself, you're more anxious and uncomfortable in your life.

It's easier to lose your balance, or your temper.

The inability to self soothe creates a life

filled with discomfort and chronic anxiety or anger.

When you can't self-soothe, it's easy to look for soothing in things like overeating, drinking too much, excessive spending or using drugs.

The chronic anxiety, lack of self-trust and poor strategies for soothing all cause you

to feel badly about yourself.

Learning how to soothe yourself in a meaningful way will help you feel good about yourself.

Real self-soothing is just like soothing a child or a pet: it's talking to the child within you, letting this part of you know that everything is going to be OK.

Everyone has a child within them.

It's the child you once were.

It lives in your psyche once you've grown up.

Self-soothing is talking to this child within you

(which can take a while to get the hang of, and for which I've included some exercises at the end of the book).

Self-soothing is making sure that this child-part of your psyche is calmed and comforted and trusts you to deal with things in a constructive, rational manner.

When you can self-soothe, you don't need to turn to dysfunctional strategies for soothing yourself, so you won't

have a reason to feel bad about yourself.

The same principle applies to reassuring yourself.

Self-reassuring is similar to self-soothing, but it's more along the lines of encouraging yourself that you can do it; that you have what it takes to succeed and to thrive.

When you're able to reassure yourself, you worry less;

when you worry less, you do better.

When you do better, you feel better about yourself.

That's how self-reassurance leads to better self-esteem.

Self-healing is also important in developing good self-esteem.

What this means is that you attend to the emotional wounds that happened in your past.

You heal the hurt child within who feels bad about him/herself and this helps you to feel better about yourself.

In order to heal the emotional wounds of the past, you have to start by facing these wounds.

Are you carrying within you any hurt, pain, fear, anger, self-doubt, self-criticism or expectations of failure, rejection or loss?

When you face the fact that you have emotional wounds, you can begin to heal these wounds.

It helps to have the support of a skilled and caring professional when you're working on healing your emotional wounds.

Working with a therapist, counselor or coach can help you face and grieve your losses; it can help you to release your anger and your pain and let go of false beliefs and expectations about yourself, others and the world.

When you engage in self-healing, you build self-confidence and self-esteem.

It's so easy to get caught up in negative self-talk.

That has to stop.

There are things you need to say to yourself on a regular basis.

None of these are negative.

Negative self-talk will only undermine your self-esteem.

To build self-esteem, look at yourself in the mirror, picture your small self looking back out at you through your eyes, and tell your child within these things:

(science has proven that repeating these affirmations changes your brain in a positive way)

"You are a being of love."

"You are lovable, just as you are."

"You have everything you need inside of you to be loved."

"You are perfectly imperfect."

"You deserve to be loved, just for who you are."

"You deserve to be accepted, just as you are, with all your faults, flaws and mistakes."

When building your self-worth, you don't

need to look to how others see you.

No matter how much another person validates you, it won't heal the emotional wounds caused by your childhood, or other parts of your life.

No matter how little another person validates you, you're still your perfectly imperfect self.

Depending on someone else's approval puts your self-worth in their hands.

You've given away the power over your sense of self.

The choice you need to make is to validate yourself.

George's story*:

George, a 40-something man, had a challenging childhood. His mother was extremely self-centered and couldn't be bothered to care for him; his father was more interested in his job than in being a parent.

George grew up not being able to see his own value. He developed a habit of being overly helpful and care-taking, especially to selfish, exploitative women.

He had a series of unhappy relationships in which he gave and gave, with women who were only too happy to take whatever they could from him. He became miserable and depleted, and eventually, he realized that there had to be a better way to live.

He came to therapy and worked on building his self-esteem. He began by seeing that the things he went through as a child weren't a reflection of his value, but in fact, an indication of his parents' failures.

He was able to face the loss of love, acceptance and protection he so desperately needed as a child, and he grieved this loss with months of tears.

He worked with the child within, giving his child-self the affirmation, acceptance and nurturing he'd always needed.

He silenced his negative self-talk, recognizing it as simply an echo of all the negative messages that came from his parents while he was growing up.

George saw that he was lovable and valuable for the man he was, and not just for what he could do for someone else.

He developed a better sense of self-confidence and self-worth, and was eventually able to let go of his compulsive care-taking with women.

One day, George met someone kind and good. He was able to be his authentic self with her. They married and had a family. George was finally happy.

Chapter 4

Being Nice

People become nice when they've learned as a child to "earn" love.

Being nice comes from the need

to get approval and validation from others.

Being nice is all about trying to please the other person.

It's making sure you meet their needs, even if that means neglecting your own needs.

It's all about taking care of the other person, even if that means being hurt or exploited.

Being nice is people-pleasing, as opposed to true kindness.

Being nice is about avoiding confrontation, for fear of disapproval or rejection.

You don't express your true feelings or needs, for fear of angering or upsetting the other person, and risking rejection.

Being nice is about always putting the other person ahead of yourself.

But being nice all the time can be exhausting.

Even when someone approves of all you're doing, it doesn't satisfy.

And most of the time, being nice causes other people to disrespect or use you.

People tend to look down on those who they perceive of as "needy" or "desperate" for attention.

So being nice all the time can become frustrating and annoying.

You can start to become angry, because it's not working the way you hoped it would.

But that's the truth about being nice.

It doesn't work.

No amount of external validation can heal the wounds of the child within.

No amount of external approval can make you feel "good enough" about yourself.

You have to take responsibility for doing these things.

Also···

when you see people as your source of self esteem, the truth is that you're just using them to meet your needs.

So being nice is insincere.

You're doing so much to please other people, but you're really just trying to get something from them.

One common form of being nice is through

co-dependency.

This is when two people get together

so both can meet
their unmet needs
of childhood.

If neither person
received the love,
care, affirmation or
validation they needed,
while growing up···

···and by the way, everyone
needs these things···

these individuals will
try to get it through
their present-day
relationships.

In co-dependency, one person has the role of the "giver."

They care-take someone else in order to find the love, nurturing, validation, etc. they didn't receive while growing up.

One person has the role of the "receiver."

They accept all this love and care-taking in the hopes that it will make up for the love and care that was missing from their childhood.

The giver and the receiver are equally lacking in the necessities of childhood, but they have different approaches for obtaining these things.

In some co-dependent relationships, one person is always the

giver and the other is always the receiver,

but both are engaging in co-dependency to compensate for their unmet needs of their childhoods.

In many co-dependent relationships, both people take turns in the giver and receiver roles.

Some of the time, one person is "nice," and care-taking to the other; some of the time, the other person takes care of them.

The problem with co-dependency is that it doesn't work.

The giver becomes resentful because they give and they give but it never seems to make them feel good enough about themselves. (It can't.)

The receiver becomes resentful because they take and they take, but it never feels like they're getting enough love and care to compensate for what was lacking in their childhood. (It's impossible.)

Plus, the receiver becomes resentful because they feel belittled by all the care-taking (even though they wanted it and asked for it), and the giver becomes frustrated because they do so much for the receiver, but are treated with resentment.

Co-dependency inevitably leads to mutual resentment and frustration.

Like I said, it just doesn't work.

In co-dependency, being "nice" is a dance you do with someone else, but it's still about making the other person responsible for your self-esteem.

It will never lead to happiness or fulfillment.

In fact, it's quite the opposite.

So, being nice is problematic (in a lot of ways).

Most often, people will take you for granted or treat you with disrespect.

They'll take advantage
of your need to please;
they'll exploit you
at work and in love;
they'll look down on
your need for approval.

For every pleaser,
there's a user who'll
be happy to rub your
neediness in your face,
while getting what
they can from you.

For every pleaser, there's a bully, who'll pick on you, because they look down on people with low self-esteem.

Users and bullies will always be there to ask for more and more from the people-pleaser, or they'll pick on you because they see your vulnerability.

The nice person appears "weak" to the bully, because they need love and approval.

A bully is someone who, deep down inside, is extremely insecure, but they hide it well.

The bully feels threatened by the nice person, because the nice person reminds them of their own low self-esteem.

The difference is that the bully is aggressive, and they express their inadequacy through abusive behaviour.

The bully will pick on the nice person to punish them for reminding the bully that deep down, they're sorely lacking in

self-love and self-acceptance.

Sadly, the bully will never feel better by picking on the nice person.

They think that if they just do more bullying, it will eventually make them feel better about themselves.

But, more of the wrong action won't lead to the right result.

The bully can attack and attack and they'll never feel better about themselves.

No matter how humiliated they cause the nice person to feel, the bully won't build up their self-esteem.

They need to do what the rest of us do:

Learn to love themselves.

Users are an interesting group of people.

Some of them fall into the co-dependent category, in which they seek care-taking to compensate for their unmet needs for love affirmation and nurturing.

But some users are just hurtful people, who see others as merely objects.

Some users are devoid of human compassion and regard other living beings as simply tools with which they'll accomplish their aims.

Nice people are particularly vulnerable to these types of users, as their need for love and approval can blind them to the true nature of these hurtful users.

Many abusive relationships arise when a hurtful user identifies a needy nice person.

The hurtful user promises to love and validate the nice person, who then showers the user with niceness.

Even when the hurtful user becomes more and more contemptuous, exploitative, controlling

or downright cruel, the nice person might still stay with them.

This hurtful user can be a friend, a romantic partner, a parent or a boss.

The nice person will stick around, even while they're being hurt, because the user has found a way to convince them (they're

brilliant at doing this) that the pleaser can only get their needs for love and approval met by this user.

The nice person is so determined to meet their needs for love and validation that they'll tolerate disrespect and mistreatment, in order to do so.

It seems quite illogical, but it's not the logical mind of the pleaser that's involved in this decision-making process.

The nice person has been conned into believing that their source of love and approval is this hurtful user.

The longer the nice person stays with the contemptuous, abusive

user, the lower their self-esteem drops, and this only makes them feel more deserving of the mistreatment and more needy for the "love" and "approval" the hurtful user is promising.

This is how people end up in long-term abusive relationships, whether with parents, friends, romantic partners or employers.

And the answer, again, is to take responsibility for developing your own

self-love, self-acceptance, and self-care.

If you tolerate exploitation, disrespect, co-dependency, bullying, even abuse, you could develop anxiety, depression, sleep disorders or eating disorders.

You could turn to addictions, like drinking, drugs, shopping or gambling, to soothe and comfort yourself.

You could become really angry and aggravated at how you've been trying so hard to please, but it's not working out the way you hoped.

Your growing anger or frustration could

eventually push its way to the surface.

Then one of two things might happen:

Either you'll

start to leak your anger in passive-aggressive behavior,

or,

in small outbursts of rage,

or,

you'll turn to food, alcohol, drugs, or some other addictive behavior

in order to stuff down your frustration, anger and hurt feelings.

So you see being "nice" really isn't so nice.

People use you, disrespect you and even abuse you for your attempts to please.

And no matter how "nice," and pleasing you are, the truth is that you're using people for what you hope they can give you.

It's easy to become filled with negative feelings toward others

when you don't get what you hoped for.

You can become disillusioned about other people (your "illusions" about people-pleasing having been smashed).

You can become bitter and cynical and self-destructive.

Your anger can come out in self-harming or passive-aggressive behaviors,

or you can be driven to addiction, to push down your unhappiness.

You often end up feeling worse about yourself.

Being nice just doesn't work.

In fact, it backfires.

You need to let it go.

You need to be the one who's in charge of your self-worth.

You need to start

taking care of yourself.

And even if the hurtful users have convinced you of this,

there's never been anything wrong with you.

You have nothing to prove.

You deserve to be happy.

You've always deserved the best.

When your self-esteem is low, you become stuck, unable to function optimally, unable to fulfill your potential.

When you feel good about yourself, you contribute more to the world;

you give more than you take; you use fewer resources; you add more value.

Good self-esteem enables you to be more productive, constructive, loving and creative.

Good self-esteem enables you to stop using other people to validate yourself.

Good self-esteem promotes positive relationships, in that you're choosing to be with people because you like them, not because you need something from them.

Good self-esteem attracts kind, loving people to you.

Good self-esteem fosters confidence, in that you'll try more things, learn from your mistakes, achieve more success, and feel better and better about yourself.

(When you have low self-esteem, it's hard to try new things because you're full of self-doubt; i·t's hard to learn from your mistakes because the negative self-talk makes it impossible to acknowledge where you went wrong and therefore make better choices moving forward·)

Good self-esteem makes it possible for you to keep learning and growing as a person·

When you feel good about yourself,

sincerely kind, loving people are drawn to you.

When you have confidence and self-worth, bullies and users avoid you and decent people admire you.

When you let go of trying to please others, and focus on loving and accepting yourself,

you end up being loved and accepted by others, anyway.

And the haters, well, you stop caring about what they say.

The more you accept yourself, the less you care what the haters think about you. After all, they're haters!

Taking responsibility for your own self-worth

makes you happier and healthier than any attempts to obtain approval from others.

This happiness overflows outward and enables you to be there for others in a spontaneous way, very different than being "nice..."

...which brings us to being kind.

Alyssa's story*:

Alyssa was a very "nice" young professional woman. She had grown up with a hurtful mother and a father who didn't know how to protect her.

Although she was smart, capable and attractive, Alyssa felt worthless and incompetent. She came to believe that the only way to get her needs met in life was to be "nice."

Alyssa was a people-pleaser, both in the workplace and in her personal relationships but in fact, this wasn't making her happy.

In the workplace, people were disrespectful to her. They saw how eager she was to please and they took advantage of her by getting her to work late, come in on the weekends and take on extra projects.

Despite all her efforts, Alyssa was not seen as an asset to her company. Her desperate need to gain approval was looked down on and instead of being promoted or given a raise, she was exploited and sometimes even bullied at work.

In her personal life, Alyssa didn't do much better. Her niceness was seen by the men she dated as a sign that they could take advantage of her. They'd get what they wanted and then leave her, making her wonder what she did wrong.

Alyssa didn't realize that her attempts at pleasing were backfiring on her, in the workplace and in her personal life. She had to learn to stop putting other people's needs ahead of her own; she had to move from being "nice" to being kind.

Chapter 5

Being Kind

Being kind has the opposite motivation of being nice.

Being kind comes from an overflowing and outpouring of self-love onto

others.

Whereas being "nice" has an ulterior motive, being kind is its own motivation.

We're kind because we feel happy.

We're kind because our self-love and self-care enable us to have positive feelings toward others.

Nice people don't express their needs or feelings.

They don't set limits with others.

They avoid confrontation.

Kind people love and accept themselves, so they aren't worried about how they're seen by others.

They're able to ask for what they want;

they're able to express their feelings;

they're able to say, "No."

They don't get frustrated because they're not waiting for approval.

They don't get angry because they're not tolerating disrespect.

Kind people want to be there for others, but never at their own expense.

Kind people want to do the right thing for others, as well as for *themselves.*

Kind people garner a lot of respect, because they're doing good for the right reasons, and because their own self-worth sets the tone for how others treat them.

Being nice requires a lot of effort, and it results in frustration.

Being kind is effortless and it results in happiness and success.

Being kind doesn't require a lot of energy, as it's

the natural outgrowth of good self-worth.

Being kind is a state of freedom, as the kind person isn't preoccupied by how others think of them.

Being kind is a state of empowerment, because the kind person takes ownership of their sense of self.

Being nice is inauthentic, as the nice person is trying to be what they think the other

person wants them to be.

Being kind is utterly authentic; when you're kind, you're being genuine, sincere and true to yourself.

Being nice deprives you of the opportunity for intimacy, as intimacy is defined as "seeing and being seen."

The nice person is putting on a pleasing persona, so any approval they receive is for the persona, not for their true self.

The kind person is being genuine.

They're not attached to the possibility of approval or disapproval from others.

In being authentic, the kind person is available for the deepest form of intimacy with others.

The kind person knows that when someone likes or loves them, it's for who they really are.

When you're kind, you're being loved for your true self.

So, being kind enables meaningful connections with others.

In the workplace, being nice makes a person into a doormat.

They're exploited and bullied; scorned and rejected.

The kind person at work is well-liked.
Their confidence inspires those around them to do their best.

Their good self-esteem causes their staff, colleagues and supervisors to admire them and listen to them.

The kind person is appreciated because their acts of kindness, unlike those of the nice person, never come with strings attached.

The kind person, in their personal and professional relationships, takes good care of themselves.

They're warm yet honest with their friends, family and loved ones, and they're smart and strategic at work.

Kindness takes so little energy and causes so little frustration that the kind person has a lot to give.

The kind person will never be mistaken for a patsy or doormat.

If someone tries to do them harm, they

deal with it, using the minimum energy required.

The nice person is clingy, sticking to people in the hope that eventually, their need for validation will be met.

The kind person feels free to walk away from any relationship that isn't working for them.

They're willing to give the other person a

chance, if there's been a misunderstanding or a disagreement,

but they won't keep engaging in counterproductive interactions, because it's just not worth it to them.

The kind person isn't tempted to try to explain themselves to others,

whereas the nice person feels a great need to be understood.

When you're kind, you know that those who are capable of understanding you will do so,

and those who aren't capable of understanding you aren't worth bothering with.

The nice person feels helpless and out of control, a lot of the time, as their sense of self is in other people's hands.

The kind person feels empowered and relaxed, as they own their self-esteem and they feel a sense of agency in life.

The nice person does a lot for others, but it's always too much, and they end up resentful and bitter.

The kind person does a lot for others, but it's always in balance, and they remain open and cheerful.

If someone disapproves of a nice person, they're devastated.

If you're a kind person and someone disapproves of you, you see it as a reflection of that person and not about yourself.

If someone criticizes a "nice" person, it will be very hard for that person to let in what the other person is saying.

It's so painful for the approval-seeker to meet with negative feedback.

If someone criticizes the kind person, they will consider what's being said.

They'll reject criticism that's given as an attack, but they'll listen closely to that which is given constructively.

The kind person, with intact self-worth, can tolerate constructive critiques, and is pleased to learn from them.

In fact, the better the self-worth, the less "ego" a person has and the more able they are to hear feedback and really take it in.

In this way, the kind person is able to keep improving their performance at work, and keep developing in their personal relationships.

The nice person, being terrified of negative feedback, has a closed mind.

This keeps them stuck in the same place forever, or at least until they're willing to look at what's driving their behavior.

The kind person can always keep growing and changing for the better.

This makes them a better and better worker, partner, family member and friend, and it perpetuates a positive cycle of learning, improving and feeling better about themselves.

Sadly, the nice person, fearing criticism, will have a hard time learning and growing, and as a result, will have little opportunity to use this to build their own self-worth.

If you're a kind person, you love yourself as much as you love other people; you care for yourself as much as you care for other people, and you stand up for yourself as much as you stand up for other people.

Some will call you selfish" and "self-serving" for being so good to yourself, but they're missing the point.

Being kind is a "win-win" equation, in which everyone benefits.

Being nice, on the other hand, is a "lose-lose" equation, in which no-one benefits.

When you're a "nice" person, you're not taking care of yourself; you're not being yourself;

you're not giving your best to others, and you're often filled with resentment.

It's obvious, then, that the ideal way to be isn't nice; it's kind.

By using the tools
in the first three
chapters of this book,
you can transform
yourself from someone
who is "nice," and
unhappy, to someone
who is content,
connected, self-caring
and kind.

Cameron's story*:

Cameron is a 40-something tradesman who didn't grow up with good self-esteem, but he developed it by working on himself.

He had many challenges in his life, but he was able to overcome many of these challenges and gradually build a sense of self-confidence and self-acceptance.

Cameron used to be a people-pleaser, but he learned, through many upsetting experiences, that this doesn't work. He was able to shift away from being "nice" and saw, first-hand, how being kind is a win-win.

Cameron saw how being kind made him happy, because he began to consider his own needs and feelings in his interactions with others; he also saw how being kind made others happy, because he had a lot more time and energy to give to them, and he was rarely angry or frustrated.

Cameron had grown up with some high-school friends who were rude, selfish people. They continued to hang around with Cameron, mainly because he was generous with them and tolerant of their bad behaviour.

Cameron told himself that they were his oldest friends, and that he should "cut them some slack," but every time he hung out with them, he came away irritated and unhappy.

Finally, he came to see that his loyalty to himself had to come first, even before his loyalty to his old friends. He talked to the guys, letting them know what didn't work for him, and then saw how they reacted.

A couple of the men realized that the group they'd been hanging around with all these years was bringing out the worst in them, and they appreciated Cameron setting them straight. Because of Cameron's input, they were able to change their ways and could all stay friends.

Several members of the group didn't like hearing from Cameron that their behaviour wasn't working for him. They put him down and told him that they weren't going to change. They made it clear that he had to take them as they were, or he should forget about the friendship.

Fortunately, Cameron had come to respect and value himself. He knew that he deserved to be treated with a minimum of courtesy and consideration, even from his trouble-making childhood friends. He saw that anyone who expected him to put up with their bad behaviour wasn't a real friend to him.

He was sad to walk away from his old friends but he did it, knowing that there was no point in holding on to relationships that made him so unhappy.

By not exhausting and frustrating himself as a people-pleaser, and by not tolerating mistreatment, Cameron had more time and energy to put into relationships that made him happy, and he went on to make new friends, people who could accept him for exactly who he was.

Chapter 6

Nice vs. Kind in the Workplace

Most of us have to go to work.

Some of us are stuck in people-pleasing.

How does that affect us in the workplace?
One word: BADLY

People-pleasers at work are overly-conscientious and will work too hard and too long, looking for approval from their supervisors.

People-pleasers at work tend to get taken advantage of, and they often end up burnt out, resentful, or both.

If you've been a people-pleaser at work, you might have had to take time off, because of frustration and exhaustion.

Some people-pleasers end up doing a lot more work than everyone else, and are the go-to person when there's any extra work to do.

Some people-pleasers at work become so frustrated by these things that they inadvertently act out. This behaviour can sabotage their work performance and risk their career.

Some people-pleasers at work find that their bosses or colleagues are unsupportive, even unkind toward them.

Often, people-pleasers are subject to harassment or bullying.

Why do people-pleasers end up being mistreated at work?

This happens for the same reasons that "nice" people are mistreated in their personal lives:

- Some people note the pleaser's desperation for approval and look down on this;

- Some people see their own neediness reflected in the pleaser at work, and resent this person for reminding them of their own vulnerabilities;

Some people like power, and when they see a pleaser, they use this person's neediness against them.

Whatever the reason, the people-pleaser at work is often treated worse than the other employees.

This is confusing to them, as they're working extra hard to please, and can't understand why they, of all people, should be mistreated.

If you've been a people-pleaser at work, and especially if you've experienced mistreatment, you'll understand how this way of operating in the workplace just doesn't pay off.

It's important to understand that the workplace is not your family; your bosses aren't your parents and your colleagues aren't your siblings or your close friends.

You can have a warm, supportive work environment, but never confuse it with your personal life.

The workplace is where you do your job and get the satisfaction of a job well done; as well as being able to learn, be challenged, and develop mastery.

The workplace is not where you meet your emotional needs for affirmation, validation or approval·

The more you mistake your workplace for the source of these emotional needs, the more likely it is that the people at work will disrespect you, and even mistreat you·

The child within sees every environment as a substitute for family, and seeks his/her emotional gratification in each one·

It's your job to deal directly with the child within you; giving this part of your psyche all the validation, approval and affirmation he/she needs, so that the workplace is no longer seen as the source of these things.

The adult sees the workplace as where they go to work. The adult understands that the workplace will never be a source of emotional healing.

If you've been a people-pleaser at work, it's because the child within you is in charge at work, and looking for something that they can't actually find there.

If you've been trying too hard to find approval at work, you need to take responsibility for your own emotional healing, and start giving this approval to your child within.

When you've directly addressed the needs of the child within, you'll be able to be fully adult in the workplace, and not have the needy child within interfering with your success at work.

Julie's story:

Julie was a thirty-something woman who was overly-conscientious in her workplace. She came in early, left late, and always ended up doing the work that her colleagues couldn't finish.

Her boss seemed to appreciate her efforts, but when it came time for promotions, Julie was consistently passed up. This happened over and over, and Julie's boss could never give her a good explanation for why this was happening.

Eventually, Julie got into therapy, and realized that her habit of doing more work than she needed to, as well as everyone else's work made her too useful to her boss to promote out of her current environment.

Julie had effectively made herself un-promotable. She realized that she had to advocate for herself, and lobbied for a promotion, saying that she would be a valuable asset in her new role.

Finally, her boss relented and Julie took on a role with greater responsibility. However, because of her work in psychotherapy, she was able to find a balance between doing a good job and overdoing it.

Julie learned how to perform optimally so as to demonstrate her abilities, but never to make herself so indispensable to a department that her boss wouldn't want to promote her out of it.

Belinda's Story:

Belinda was a well-meaning manager in a busy company but she struggled for a long time with being too "nice." She was very uncomfortable with conflict and confrontation and therefore she wasn't able to intervene effectively when problems arose with her staff members.

Belinda had always hoped that the workers would sort things out on their own so that she wouldn't be forced into a confrontation with anyone or be seen as "taking sides." Unfortunately, her discomfort with conflict and her need to be seen as "nice" by her staff made her a very ineffective manager.

Belinda had one employee who'd been demonstrating over time an overly-entitled attitude and who had started shirking their work. The other staff members were becoming upset about the unfair situation in their workplace and unbeknownst to Belinda, staff morale was beginning to deteriorate.

The frustrated co-workers were taking more sick days from work, and even when they were in the office, they weren't being as efficient or productive as usual. Meanwhile, the entitled worker came in a few minutes late every day, left a few minutes early, and spent several hours at work surfing the net or sending personal emails.

Belinda was so invested in avoiding conflict that she was in denial about the lowered productivity in her workplace. She chose to take on extra work herself, to compensate for the work that wasn't being done by the people who were actually responsible for it.

In addition, Belinda gave extra work to a few employees who were also overly "nice," and these workers became saddled with the tasks that their colleagues were supposed to be attending to. Belinda was becoming burnt out and her overworked fellow "nice" staffers became more and more resentful.

Arguments began breaking out between the workers, as their anger grew toward the one individual who'd been getting away with not doing their job. The staff members were also becoming exasperated with Belinda, whom they felt was avoiding the problem.

What's the answer to a problem like this? It's simple. Belinda needed to develop some confidence and some tools around becoming an effective manager. She needed to understand that being seen as "nice" couldn't be her priority in her role as manager.

She also needed to learn practical skills for handling lazy or toxic work staff. She had to see that everyone loses when a manager doesn't address these types of staff issues, and that everyone wins when the manager steps in and confronts the problem head-on.

A kind manager assesses the situation and deals with it, regardless of how the staff might view her, or how the one lazy worker might feel toward her. A kind manager thinks of the wellness and productivity of her entire office and staff, rather than worrying about being liked.

Paradoxically, the more concerned Belinda was with her reputation, the less effective she was as a manager, and the more the staff members ended up resenting her. In the end, her attempts to be liked backfired on her; office productivity was at an all-time low, and Belinda had

begun contemplating sick leave for burn-out. All of this could have been avoided if Belinda had prioritized being kind over being "nice."

///

All the people in the above stories have been in therapy with me. In order to protect their confidentiality, their names and any identifying details about them have been changed; some of the people depicted are composites of more than one person. Although changed, the stories are true to the spirit of their experiences.

Exercises

Here are some tools that you can use, after you've read this book.

1: Mindfulness exercise

Begin to pay attention to all the times you engage in negative self-talk, either silently in your head or out loud, in front of other people.

Start to catch yourself as you're saying these negative things and then rephrase them. When you hear yourself saying that you're "stupid," or that you've just "blown it," or that you're "an idiot;" that you can't do something or you don't deserve it; that you're not as good as the other person or that you'll never make it; that you "should" do something for someone else or that you shouldn't ask for help, STOP and change that to something positive, or at least something much less self-critical.

In your own head, you can say, "No, we're not going there," when you hear self-critical statements. You can say to yourself, "Oh, that's a lie," or "Nothing good will come from believing this," or "Let's change this script," and then you can replace the negative statement with something much more affirming and much less critical.

If you've made a mistake or fallen short in front of others, you can say to them (and in your head), "Oops, I made a mistake here," or, "I'm sorry about that," or "Right, I see what you mean about that," without ever having to put yourself down. We're all human and imperfect.

Try to do this exercise every time you find yourself being overly self-critical, and you'll begin to break this bad habit of negative self-talk.

2: Letting go of other people's version of you/ owning your greatness

It's natural to believe that how others saw you, described you or reacted to you when you were growing up is really a reflection of you. Looking back, you can see that such a negative response wasn't about you at all, but rather a reflection of the people around you.

To counter feelings of inadequacy or low self-worth, you can spend time every day affirming who you really are by doing the affirmations in this book and by telling yourself:

"I am myself. No-one else can tell me who I am. I don't have to take on anything from anybody else. I know my value. My value isn't defined by anyone else. No matter how other people treat me, I know that I'm valuable and capable and deserving of love and respect."

3: Being productive, constructive, active and connected

One of the best ways to feel good about yourself is to live your life more fully; to engage in projects and activities that are creative, productive and meaningful.

Think about the things that make you happy, ener-
gized and excited; things that make you feel alive. These
are things to do by yourself—it's empowering to be able to
create something all by yourself—and things to do in col-
laboration with other, like-minded individuals—working
together toward a common goal is deeply satisfying.

Being physically active builds self-esteem. This isn't
about getting the "beautiful body" or the "super-strong
body," but rather, feeling alive in your body with head,
heart and body connected and integrated. Feeling good in
your body helps you to feel good about yourself.

Being creative makes you feel empowered and positive.
Doing art on your own gives you a tremendous sense of
accomplishment and control, when you can say, "I did this
myself!" Doing creative projects with others gives you a
strong sense of belonging; you're part of a creative community. All this will boost your sense of self-worth.

Engaging in activities that benefit other people, ani-
mals, your own community and other communities further afield will boost your self-esteem. You'll feel that
you're making a positive contribution and it's a real win-
win. You'll feel great and others will benefit.

Connecting to kind, loving people builds self-esteem.
Spending time with others; helping each-other out, learning about each-other and the world, laughing together,
building things together, all these things will boost your
self-worth and give you a sense of belonging in the world.

Connection isn't about depending on others for your
identity or self-esteem; it's about how sharing love and
support builds everyone up.

Being connected to others makes life more meaningful. It gives you an opportunity to demonstrate caring and compassion. This automatically makes you feel better about yourself.

4: Working with the child within

I've found that it's very helpful to take time every day to do your "inner work." It may sound silly but the best way I've found to help people connect to the child within is for them to go out and purchase an "inner child doll" or stuffed animal that represents their child self.

Once you've got your doll or stuffed animal, you need to see it as "little you," and start sitting with this "mini me" and talking to him/her.

You start by affirming the child and telling him/her how wonderful, adorable, precious and lovable he/she is. Then you acknowledge his/her hurts, wounds and losses, and start to grieve them.

Obviously, the tears will be coming out of your eyes, but it will feel like the child is grieving his/her own past hurts and losses. You hold the doll/stuffed animal and soothe the child within, telling him/her that you're sorry for what he/she had to go through; that he/she never deserved it; that you're here for him/her now, and that you love him/her and will protect him/her, from now on.

Another important aspect of the inner work is reassuring and soothing the child within; telling him/her that it's okay; you're here now to take care of him/her; that he/she can do it; that those mean people aren't telling the truth; that he/she is lovable, deserving and smart.

Finally, you sit with the child doll/stuffed animal and you listen for the negative self-talk. You identify and reject all the negativity you can, and you affirm the child as much as you can. This will create self-trust—the child within will trust you to protect him/her and will be more willing to cooperate with you, rather than resisting your attempts at positive change.

When the child within trusts you to take care of him/her, protect him/her, soothe and reassure him/her, you'll never be at odds with yourself. You'll never find yourself knowing that you ought to do something but for some reason, you're unable to follow through with it. When the child within trusts you, they'll go along with your plans, and you'll never have an "inner conflict" that keeps you from doing what you need to do to live your best life and be your best self.

6: Attributes of the "nice" person, and attributes of the kind person

The nice person:

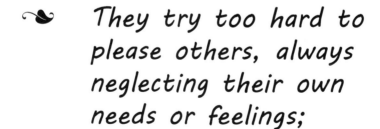 *They try too hard to please others, always neglecting their own needs or feelings;*

- *They overwork-whether at home, school or their job-trying to win approval;*

- *They're overly conscientious and spend more time and effort than everyone else on a project, to make sure they "got it right;"*

- *They're preoccupied with how others view them;*

- *They care-take others;*

- *They're unable to say, "No," or to set limits on other peoples' hurtful behaviour toward them;*

- *They become extremely distressed if they feel they've made a mistake;*

- *They can't tolerate criticism, as it devastates them to have fallen short;*

- *They avoid conflict and tend to be placating to bullies and overly tolerant of mistreatment;*

- *They can become resentful that they're doing so much for others and not receiving the validation they were hoping for;*

- *They can become passive-aggressive, if the resentment leaks out;*

- *They tend to neglect their own well-being in favour of doing for others.*

The kind person:

- *They give to others out of a feeling of inner fullness, not expecting anything in return;*

- *They're able to say "No" and set appropriate limits on other peoples' behaviour;*

- *They stand up for themselves as much as for others;*

- *They are good at "healthy confrontation," expressing their needs and feelings clearly and honestly;*

- *They aren't preoccupied with how others see them;*

- *They feel love and concern for others but won't exhaust or deplete themselves to be helpful;*

- *They're self-motivated, and their actions come*

out of their true wants
and needs;

- They never enable bad
behaviour by others;

- They feel empowered to
walk away from those
who are hurtful or
disrespectful to them;

- They understand that
love never means
allowing others to be
hurtful.

I'd love to hear from you!

Contact me at:

info@marciasirotamd.com

Made in the USA
Lexington, KY
26 October 2018